# In the Arms
# of Angels

# In the Arms of Angels

## Messages from the Angelic Realms
## to Help You on Your Way

Claire Nahmad
with illustrations and angel blessings
by Olwen Ballantyne

WATKINS PUBLISHING
LONDON

This edition first published in the UK and USA 2012 by
Watkins Publishing, Sixth Floor, Castle House,
75–76 Wells Street, London W1T 3QH

Design and Typography Copyright © Watkins Publishing 2012
Text Copyright © Claire Nahmad 2012
Illustrations Copyright © Olwen Ballantyne 2012
Calligraphy Copyright © Don Makin 2012

1 3 5 7 9 10 8 6 4 2

Designed by Jerry Goldie

Printed and bound in Malaysia for Imago

British Library Cataloguing-in-Publication Data Available

Library of Congress Cataloging-in-Publication Data Available

ISBN: 978-1-78028-379-1

www.watkinspublishing.co.uk

Distributed in the USA and Canada by Sterling Publishing Co., Inc.
387 Park Avenue South, New York, NY 10016-8810

For information about custom editions, special sales, premium and
corporate purchases, please contact Sterling Special Sales
Department at 800-805-5489 or specialsales@sterlingpub.com

# CONTENTS

To my beloved husband Steve
for the journey we have shared;

to our sons Merick and Justin, with every blessing;

to my parents, Jack and Daphne Jones, for their love
and support.

*Olwen*

We would like to dedicate this book to Jenny Parkin,
with out heartfelt thanks and appreciation. Thank you
for being our 'angel', Jenny.

# ACKNOWLEDGEMENTS

Thank you, Steve Ballantyne, my beloved husband, for all your support and for peacefully accepting our home filling up with angels and their transcribed messages.

Blessings and thanks to our sons Merick and Justin; you will always be our lovely boys.

Thank you to my parents, Daphne and Jack Jones, for always doing their best for me.

A heartfelt thank you to our gorgeous friend, Elma Cordiner, for her enthusiasm and support on this journey, and most especially for buying my first angel painting, 'Spirit in the Sky'.

Thank you to our lovely friend, Janice Edie, for all her gentle reminders about patience.

Thank you to our generous friends, Margaret and Bill Paterson, for all their hospitality.

Thank you to Margaret Wilson, who will always be our special neighbour, no matter where she lives.

Thank you, Lisa Buchannan, for your beautiful photographs of my paintings.

Thank you, Don Makin, for the gift of your stunning calligraphy and for your boundless enthusiasm.

Huge thanks also to the beautiful circle of people who have my angels and their messages in their homes; how blessed we all are to be part of this ongoing miracle.

Last but not least, thank you, Claire, for your beautiful writing and your strength of purpose. You are a magnificent inspiration. Well done.

*Olwen*

Thanks to Olwen for giving me the opportunity to collaborate with her on this book.

*Claire*

# OLWEN

# AND THE ANGELS

The idea for this book suggested itself when Olwen Ballantyne made contact with me and sent me a selection of her angel paintings. These paintings decidedly carry angelic frequencies. I was amazed to find that, invariably, looking at the painted angels would lift an oppressive mood or a heavy atmosphere within minutes (curiously, about the same amount of time that an analgesic takes to work ... although the word does contain 'angels'!).

The remarkable story of how the angels made contact with Olwen and requested that she should give them material form through her artwork and convey their essence through her words is a simple and a beautiful one. On 3 September 2004, a miracle occurred. Suddenly, as Olwen was working on a painting, the air around her became alive with angelic presence. The first message and the first angelic image were given to her from the heart of this vibrancy, and since then, Olwen has painted several hundred angels.

Each painting has always been accompanied by an outflow of words, a shining linguistic vessel containing the harmonic frequencies of angelic consciousness, given to us as a gift through Olwen from her angel friends, so that we might lift our own perception into attunement with the angels and transform our lives and our world. The images and the words work together to open channels within us whereby we experience angelic communion and break free of the shackles which imprison us in the mundane sphere of the material world.

The angels sing to us the ancient Song Celestial in silent voices, and we receive it as an ineffable pulse which revivifies us from beyond the stars, from beneath the configurations of our thoughts. It comes to us from the heart of the Divine, and it is the life-breath, the life-blood, of our higher selves.

Having experienced angelic attunement since I was a child, I was particularly drawn to the dynamics of the angel messages existing within the design of Olwen's paintings. Ever recreating themselves anew by merging with the individual perception of the observer, Olwen's images seem mystically wired to bring us the revelation our soul needs at any given time. This is indeed the true angel language, because angels speak to us in colours and symbols. It may be helpful to remember that angels *hear* colours and *see* sounds (which take beautiful symbolic form in their world). The colours Olwen selects are radical and arresting, rich as caskets of jewels. They are sonorous but not loud, abundant but not clamorous. They are fluid statements conveyed to us from beings of the angelic realms, intimating to us something of their vivid and fecund worlds and inviting us to join them there, even whilst we live our lives in mortal bodies and mortal conditions here on earth. We do not have to be bound, oppressed or limited by our bodies and our environment; we can choose, instead, to rise to supernal heights, lifted on the wings of our loving angel friends, who, as we enter deeper and deeper into communion with them, we will come to know so well.

Many people flock to see Olwen's paintings and, although she is a very private person, she welcomes every avid angel viewer! She recognizes that her great task in life is to initiate communion between the angelic and earthly realms, and that each person needs to connect with the angels, according to their own unique vision and soul purpose. She says:

> Angels are here to light up the universe with their essence of love and peace and joy. They are especially here to light up our own world, so that we can see what needs to be done to bring peace and love and safety, health and joy, to the whole of Mother Earth and all her children.

I think that Olwen's angels are delightful, that they are both immediate and vital in their reality, and that they encompass the themes which particularly trouble and confuse people today, bringing short, simple, healing answers which glow with angelic essence. I believe that it will soon become obvious to anyone who works with these images that they have been vividly put in touch with angels.

_Claire_

# COMMUNING WITH ANGELS

With regard to Olwen's angel paintings and messages, the work of angelic communion has already been done for us. The angels speak directly to us through them, and we are required to do nothing other than to effortlessly receive these communications as our own. However, having once begun to experience the enchantment of listening to the angels, it is only natural to wish to continue our interaction by developing our own personal contact with them.

Communing with angels is a simple and harmonious process. It is achieved by a gentle focus on the breath, and by withdrawing the mind from the activity of the outer world so that it rests in stillness in the heart. Just allow the driving force of the mind to sink softly into the heart centre, and to be absorbed by the point of peace that dwells therein. To facilitate this, we need only breathe gently and easily for a few moments, focusing on each incoming and outgoing breath with a relaxed concentration, until we feel our heart-consciousness beginning to open like a flower.

We can do this at any time and anywhere, as long as the mind is not engaged with a specific task. As we begin to enjoy regular communion with the angels, we will come to recognize a busyness in the mind which likes to dictate to us, and which will, therefore, continually supersede the will of our deeper and wiser being, if it is allowed to do so. This chattering energy in the mind, which the angels call the mind of earth, seeks to keep us bound to mundane reality and purposely obscures our recognition of those profounder and more significant worlds of spiritual reality which lie beneath the surface of everyday awareness.

As the mind of earth gains dominion, we become trapped in a daily pettifog of earthbound perception, where only the trivial and the mundane seem real. When this happens, the human soul quickly becomes frustrated, angry, fearful and stressed, because we cannot live happily and healthily, or fulfill our true potential, under such harrowing and unnatural conditions.

Communing with angels is a powerful and simple method of mastering the mind of earth, so that it can no longer assume dictatorship and hide from us the inestimable treasures of the worlds within.

The angels themselves actively seek to help us gain such mastery. Via our friendship and association with them, they reconnect us with our deeper perception so that we may live our lives joyfully, centred in the strength of our true being, rather than finding ourselves constantly cut off from it and therefore forced to endure all the suffering and fear that is the inevitable result of such alienation.

When seeking to contact our heart centre (which from a spiritual perspective is situated at the mid-point of the chest, rather than slightly to the left, which is the location of the physical organ), we need to take care that we do not miss our aim and place our awareness in the solar-plexus centre instead. The solar plexus centre, just below the heart, is fed by our desires and by our egotistical, nervous and intellectual energies. These energies are necessary to enable us to pursue our path through life, but they are certainly not the source of wisdom! If we contact this centre instead of the heart, we will no doubt experience a flow of consciousness which tells us exactly what we want to hear, but it will not be angelic voices which communicate with us, but rather a misleading voice emanating from our own desires – what some people call the 'daydream voice'!

The solar-plexus centre is characterized by its eager, rushing, torrential energy. It tends to speak to us either seductively or impatiently.

Whichever masquerade it chooses, it is not the true angelic voice received in the heart.

The energies of the heart are those of an exalted consciousness. Their atmosphere is calm, pure, clear and stable, rooted and grounded in a serene and mighty strength and in an unassailable silence. The essence of the heart is love centred in peace, and it is from this point of peace within that we will hear the angels speak to us.

*Claire*

# Angel Messages

# SPIRIT IN THE SKY

*G*et ready to expand and acknowledge that we are
one with the Spirits in the Sky, and that they
are one with us.

✳

The love that is here for us on Mother Earth at the present
moment is phenomenal.

✳

We are being enfolded by the higher energies of the Spirits
in the Sky during this time of change.

✳

It is wonderful to access the joy that this knowledge brings,
and give thanks.

*Olwen*

# SPIRIT IN THE SKY

Get ready to expand and acknowledge
that we are
one with the Spirits in the Sky,
and they are one with us.

The Love that
is here for us on
Mother Earth
at the present
moment is
phenomenal.
We are being
enfolded by the
higher energies of the Spirits in
the Sky during this time of change

It is wonderful to access
the joy that this knowledge
brings, and give thanks.

*S*pirit in the Sky was the first angel painting, and the first angel message, that Olwen received on that eventful and wonderful evening of 3 September 2004, when the angels suddenly made contact with her.

It is a beautiful reminder that the angels use the element of air to draw close to us. The angels enter us through the medium of air. We absorb their influences, their very essence, through the magical act of breathing ... for our breath is indeed magical and sacred. This is a lesson of light that the angels teach us.

They would also teach us another source of joy – the art of dancing. Today, we often constrain our dancing within social, professional and sexually orientated parameters. The angels would have us throw off such shackles, and dance freely upon the earth, with no purpose other than to express delight. The angels, the sylphs, the Spirits in the Sky, will show us how to unbind ourselves through dance.

We all breathe the same air, the freely circulating, equalizing air of brotherhood.

Breathe in the angels!

Dance!

*Claire*

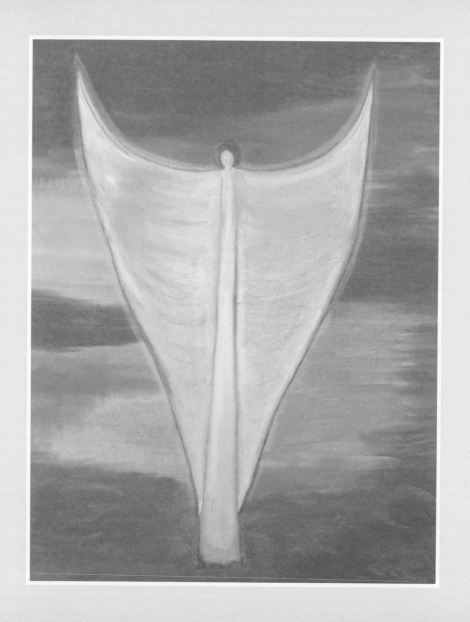

# ENCOMPASS

*T*his Angel encompasses all the wonderful things that the word Angel brings to mind: love, peace support, joy, eternal. There is also another side to this Angel, which is asking us to open ourselves to encompassing all the good words that we feel we can apply to Angels, and to increase them in our own lives.

As I'm writing this, the phrases 'non-judgemental acceptance' and 'from the bottom, top, front, side and middle of our hearts' have come clearly into my mind. So let's do better, let's love more deeply, let's judge less harshly, let's feel peace more regularly, let's support more often, let's accept people as they are more readily, and let's increase the joy we experience and share daily.

Let us truly centre ourselves and start to live our lives as earth Angels.

✶

# Encompass

This Angel encompasses all the wonderful things that the word Angel brings to mind, love, peace, support, joy, eternal.

There is also another side to this Angel, which is asking us to open ourselves to encompassing all the good words that we feel we can apply to Angels, and to increase them in our own lives.

As I'm writing this the phrases non-judgemental acceptance, and from the bottom, top, front, side and middle of our hearts have come clearly into my mind.

So let's do better, lets love more deeply, lets judge less harshly, lets feel peace more regularly, lets support more often, lets accept people as they are more readily, and lets increase the joy we experience and share daily.

Let us truly centre ourselves and start to live our lives as earth Angels.

This angel is guiding us towards encompassing life
as it is; to let go of 'we did this wrong' or, 'they didn't
do things right' ...
... Time to encompass the knowledge that it was all
happening perfectly, and that it all still is ...
When we accept the good, the bad and the indifferent as part
of life's rich pattern, when we accept that life holds darkness
as well as light, we can then release the pain we cling to
through rejecting the dark.
The dark and the shadow sides are to teach us lessons
about increasing our light. When we embrace these lessons
without resistance, we can release the darkness they bring
us and be free to enjoy the encompassing light.

*Olwen*

*T*he Encompassing Angel is often associated with our own Guardian Angel, an angelic being specially assigned to each one of us, who will accompany us from the instant of conception throughout every moment of our lives, and will be there to lift us over the threshold at the time of our passing.

Our Guardian Angel teaches us lessons about the darkness as well as the light, always showing us how the darkness can be transformed into light, and that there is no need to be afraid of it.

I have adapted an ancient prayer from the Western Isles of Scotland, where a deeply established fund of spiritual wisdom and a highly developed awareness of angels once existed. This prayer can be said each night as a method of invoking angelic protection.

# The Guardian Angel

Thou Guardian Angel who hast charge of me,
Sent by the mercy of the Great Spirit,
Encompass me in thy circle of perfect light,
Enfold me in thy fragrant wings.

Drive from me every temptation and danger,
Surround me on the sea of unrighteousness,
And in the narrows, crooks and straits,
Keep thou my coracle, keep it always.

Be thou a bright flame before me,
Be thou a guiding star above me,
Be thou a smooth path below me,
And be a kindly shepherd behind me,
Today, tonight, and forever.

Lead thou me to the land of angels;
Lead thou me to my true and radiant home,
To the Court of the Lightener of the Stars,
To the white peace of heaven.

*Claire*

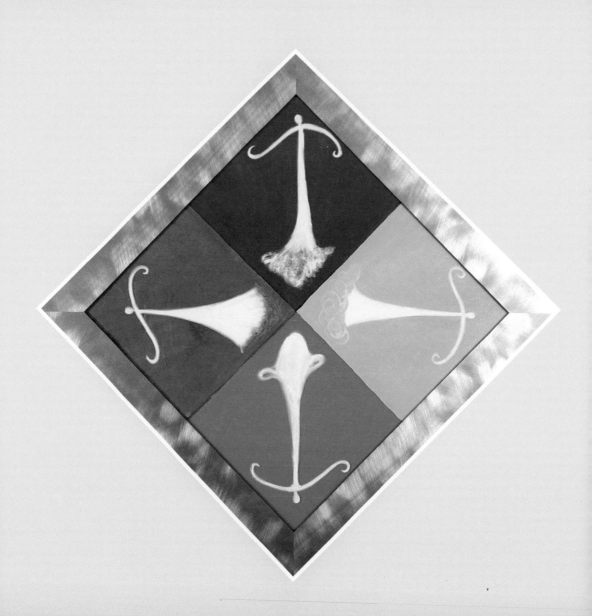

# FOUR CORNERS

This is about Angels, in all their glory, being in every 'corner' of the world, there for all races, colours and creeds. Are we mad, though, thinking of the earth having corners, boundaries, divisions? Mother Earth is round, seamless, devoid of divides. These are made by man.

✳

Let's hold hands around the world and make it a place of Love and Peace and Joy. The corners are all in our mind. It's time to release them.

✳

We are brothers and sisters, we are one, and we live together on this corner-free planet.

*Olwen*

This is about Angels in all their glory being in every corner of the World, there for all races, colours and creeds.

Are we mad though, thinking of the earth having corners, boundaries, divisions. Mother Earth is round, seamless, devoid of divides. These are made by man.

## FOUR CORNERS

We are brothers and sisters, we are One, and we live together on this corner-free planet.

Let's hold hands around the world, and make it a place of Love and Peace and Joy. The corners are all in our mind. It's time to release them.

*T*he four great archangels of the cardinal points are:

- Michael, Lord of Fire and the Southern Gate;
- Gabriel, Lord of Water and the Western Gate;
- Uriel, Lord of Earth and the Northern Gate;
- Raphael, Lord of Air and the Eastern Gate.

These archangels bear a feminine as well as a masculine aspect, and, indeed, they are sourced in a sacred feminine essence. We can call on them and receive their gifts; the angels ask of us only that we freely share such gifts.

Attune to these mighty archangels by withdrawing into inner quietude and focusing on the heart centre and the gentle rhythm of the incoming and outgoing breath. As you call on each archangel, intone its name softly, like a chant, until you feel the descent of an encircling spiritual presence.

To call on Archangel Michael, become aware of the space to your right. Michael may be summoned for protection, enlightenment, cleansing, forgiveness, and the power of universal love and truth. Bathe in her-his golden presence, and summon Michael's purifying fires to rise upwards from your feet in a column of spiritual flame to rid your soul of its darkness and limitations.

To call on Archangel Gabriel, become aware of the space behind you. See this archangel as a torrent of purest water containing living light. Archangel Gabriel brings inspiration, revelation and freedom from fear. Let this mighty archangel wash through you in a sweeping surge of purification and revivification. Release your fears and take back your power and your centredness, so that your soul is restored to you in its fullest measure.

To call on Archangel Raphael, become aware of the space before you. Archangel Raphael holds the power of healing, of making whole. Breathe in the healing magic that this great archangel emanates, and let yourself be healed at every level. Feel the healing flow gently encompass your physical body, your mental body and your emotional body. Be healed, be whole and enter into harmony.

To call on Archangel Uriel, become aware of the space to your left. Archangel Uriel wields the power of clarity, of sudden illumination, of dynamism; and yet Uriel gives forth peace. Ask for and receive her-his gifts of discernment and discrimination, of wise decision-making and of ineffable peace, the fragrant breath of heaven.

Be aware of all four archangels, of the angels of the four corners, and then see a ring of pure and perfect light encircling all. You may like to make use of this ancient charm for angelic attunement and the blessing of the archangels:

> Before me Raphael,
> Behind me Gabriel,
> At my right hand, Michael,
> At my left hand, Uriel;
> Around and about us
> The peace and protection of heaven,
> The white wings of the angels,
> The eternal ring of God.

*Claire*

# STAIRWAY

*I*sn't it wonderful,
and such a comfort to know,
that we are on our stairway to heaven?

✳

Angels will be with us
all the way,
supporting us
with their
Divine Love!

*Olwen*

STAIRWAY

Isn't it wonderful,
and such a comfort to know,
that we are on our stairway
to heaven,

Angels will be with us
all the way

supporting us

with their

Divine Love!

*T*he angel meditation that follows is designed to cleanse and revitalize the chakra system. Chakras are points within our physical being which connect us to the spiritual worlds, and are associated with the ductless glands.

We have seven main chakras which are located at:

- the base of the spine;
- a central point a little below the navel, known as the sacral chakra and linked to the spleen;
- the solar plexus;
- the heart;
- the throat (in its hollow);
- between and just above the eyes on the brow ridge, known as the third eye;
- the crown.

The crown chakra is a double chakra and expresses itself not only in the traditional location of the crown but also at the midpoint of the forehead, which I like to refer to as the unicorn's horn chakra. There is also an eighth chakra, which is situated just below our feet.

The chakras each have their own individual colours, which do not correspond to the colours of the rainbow, as is sometimes erroneously suggested, although the colour systems of each are linked. The chakras are disk-shaped and are formed from petal-shaped structures, like flowers. When their energy is pure and unobstructed, the disks begin to spin, releasing a fountainhead of spiritual forces which spiral upwards.

These disk and spiral shapes are microcosms of the great galaxy systems which form our universe.

Each human being is an individual universe in miniature and carries within him- or herself a perfect reflection in every detail of the entire cosmos.

The angels contact us, first through our heart chakra, and then via our chakra system. Your angels will tend to favour certain individual chakras when they communicate with you. As you work through this meditation, you will sense which of your particular chakras are most open and sensitive to angel communication. At the close of the meditation, there is an instruction to 'seal your centres'. These centres refer to the chakras. Just see in your mind's eye a cross of bright silver light encircled by a ring of light, and place it imaginally over each chakra, like a seal.

*Claire*

# STAIRWAY TO HEAVEN

Begin to breathe peacefully, through the heart, until the door to the Silence opens and you are admitted therein.

You are standing upon the good earth, under an open sky, looking up at the blue heavens.

A crystal stairway of supernatural beauty winds in a spiral from the earth up into the celestial blue. Up and down this wondrous stairway, angels of radiant loveliness and mystical presence come and go.

As you watch them in wonder, you see that there are seven great steps which compose this magnificent crystal stairway.

The stairway gleams, sometimes as pure and translucent as a diamond, and sometimes with a bright white purity as it reflects the brilliance of the angels.

You set your feet upon the first stair.

You see an angel of Earth, calm and lovely, moving towards you. She is red-cloaked and radiant, a marvel to behold. You know that she is Sophia, Angel of Wisdom.

She carries a ruby in her hand, and she places it in your first chakra, at the base of your spine. The ruby begins to glow a beautiful, clear red, like the heart of a volcano seen through a spirit-bright mirror, and your base chakra opens like a flower and begins to spin. You see the crystal stair beneath your feet shine with this wonderful, jewel-clear red, as beautiful as if it flowed like a secret joy from enchanted lands.

As the crystal stair shines beneath you, bathe in the colour; breathe it in.

'Your base chakra is cleansed and balanced, and blessed by the Angels. Stability is yours,' your companion tells you. You feel her great, rooted strength as she withdraws.

You set your feet upon the second stair.

Another angel approaches, this time a sweet, peaceful angel of Water. She is Sachael, Graceful One of the Waters.

She bears a magical, faceted gem of carnelian, glowing with the rapturous orange of a glorious summer sun sinking in a lake of red fire in the western skies. She places it in your sacral chakra, a little below your navel. The carnelian begins to pour all its vivid, vital orange and fiery red into your sacral chakra, so that this second centre opens like a flower and begins to spin. You see the crystal stair beneath your feet light up with this scintillating orange and crimson red.

As the crystal stair shines beneath you, bathe in the colours; breathe them in.

'Your sacral chakra is cleansed and balanced, and blessed by the Angels. Peace and wisdom be with you,' says Sachael of the Waters as she withdraws, leaving you as if in a great calm ocean of peace and deep inner knowing.

You set your feet upon the third stair.

You see an angel of Air approach you, with luminous flowing garments of softest blue streaming around her. She is Anael, Divine Protectress of Air, bearing a glittering jewel of yellow topaz, and a piece of precious jade with a pearly green translucence like a wave of the sea. She places both jewels in your solar plexus centre.

The topaz takes brilliant, flashing flame and the jade shimmers with the green dusky light of reflected suns as your solar plexus centre opens like a flower and begins to spin. You see the crystal stair beneath your feet light up with this coruscating yellow, this green, dim, opalescent fire, softly auriferous.

As the crystal stair shines beneath you, bathe in the colours; breathe them in.

'Your solar plexus chakra is cleansed and balanced, and blessed by the Angels. May you know the mystery of Love, both human and divine,' says the Angel Anael, brilliant in her ariel beauty. She smiles, leaving you with her angelic blessing of love as she withdraws.

You set your feet upon the fourth stair.

This time, a glowing angel of Fire, like a perfect, poised flame, draws near. She is the mighty Shekinah, Angel of Purest Everlasting Light. She carries an emerald of deep, luscious, light-filled green, secret in its depths with the wisdom of ancient sunlit forests and the life-bearing primal ocean. She places this precious jewel in her own heart centre.

'What do you see?' she asks.

You see a Being of Light in her heart, greater than the universe. You know that this is the Dragon Queen, that we are all her Children of Light, and that each of us bears a drop of her essence in our deepest heart. It is the Divine Source.

You hear yourself say, 'I see the true centre.'

'You have answered well,' says the Angel Shekinah. Her outline coruscates with holy fire; you see that she herself manifests the form of the Dragon Queen, Giver of Purest

Everlasting Light, and that she, Shekinah, is its Shepherdess.

Shekinah holds forth a jewel in each hand, flashing in the centre of her palms. One is a citrine of calm, clear, radiant gold; the other is a light-filled garnet of a brilliant wine-red. She places both jewels in your heart centre. In their radiant glow, your heart chakra opens like a flower and begins to spin. You see the crystal stair beneath your feet reflect these glorious colours and ray them out to the world as a wondrous red-gold.

As the crystal stair shines beneath you, bathe in the colour; breathe it in.

'Your heart chakra is cleansed and balanced, and blessed by the Angels,' says the majestic and gracious Shekinah. 'May the Love which unites all in brotherhood never grow dim within you.'

She leaves you as if in a miraculous cloak of all-enfolding brotherhood as she withdraws.

You set your feet upon the fifth stair. An angel of the Higher Ethers floats tranquilly to your side, shining with a mystical purity. She is an Angel of the Hidden Worlds, with a hidden name.

She places one jewel of fiery gold and another of pure, deep amethyst in your throat chakra, at the hollow of your throat. Within the rays of that mystery of gold and violet, your throat chakra opens like a flower and begins to spin. You see the crystal stair beneath your feet flood with these colours and surround you as if with an aura.

As the crystal stair shines beneath you, bathe in the colours; breathe them in.

'Your throat chakra is cleansed and balanced, and blessed by the Angels. May you know divine union,' says the Angel of the Hidden Name, leaving you with a feeling of great expanse, as if you trod the unlimited fields of space: space fields filled with light, love, warmth and joy.

You place your feet upon the sixth stair. A glittering Sun angel, brilliant and lovely, moves to your side and reveals a jewel in her palm which shines as if it were a tiny stolen piece of the sublime spiritual worlds when they shine through the mystery of the dawn; a perfect sphere of most holy rose, fragrant and alive like the bloom itself.

The angel is Gazardiel, Angel of the Rising Sun, and she places the living wonder of the rose gem in your brow chakra, which opens like a flower and begins to spin, glowing with a deep rose hue of measureless beauty, which is reflected in the crystal stair beneath your feet.

As the crystal stair shines beneath you, bathe in the colour, breathe it in.

'Your brow chakra is cleansed and balanced, and blessed by the Angels. Your third eye, the Abode of Joy, is open. May you be deeply blessed in your seeing,' says Gazardiel, Angel of the Morning; and as she withdraws, you feel a surge of joy in your newly awakened state.

You place your feet upon the seventh stair. A mighty angel of the Sun, Brigid the White herself, approaches you on a white horse. Archangel Brigid shimmers pure white and glorious gold before you, beautiful as the sanctified mind of God. She passes her hands over your head in blessing and places a pearl of peerless beauty in the crown centre at the top of your head. She opens her other hand and delivers a second pearl to the crown chakra in the middle of your forehead at the top, a pearl with a sparkling, fairy-like sheen that, like Keats' dove of hope, fills the air with silver glitterings. Your crown chakras open like two perfect flowers and begin to spin, pouring forth a transcendent pearly light like a miracle, in which a silver lustre dances like a spirit. It illumines and floods the crystal stair under your feet.

As the crystal stair shines beneath you, bathe in the colour; breathe it in.

'Your crown centres are cleansed and balanced, and blessed by the Angels,' Brigid the White, Angel of the Magnificence of the Sun, says to you. 'It is forever protected by me, and by my spiritual sword.'

Taking her sword of platinum gold from its diamond scabbard, she points upward.

'Behold, dear child of the pure and everlasting Light,' she says to you. 'You will see a vision, and experience a wonder. You are about to cross the Rainbow Bridge.'

Above her pointing sword shines the great Star, all peace, all love, the Light of the World. It is the Star that also shines within your own heart centre.

Within its heart dwells Allea, the Great Angel of the Rainbow, and from the white light pouring from the Star she creates the delicate hues of the rainbow, angel colours, many-splendoured with colours rising on scales of light into profundities of spiritual life where you cannot follow, although you can sense these transcendental colours and their sublime inner voyage at the very farthest reaches of your subtlest, intuitive vision. They are expressions of eternal Love.

Become aware, now, of your own individual Star, shining in your heart centre. Gently carry your breath to it, and breathe through it. It grows as you focus on it.

From the wondrous rose which blooms at the centre of the Star in your heart, an arched bridge, seven-hued and seven rayed, emerges. The arch of this miraculous rainbow reaches right into the centre of the great Star above, and you see that Allea, the Angel of the Rainbow at the midpoint of that great star, is actually creating one half, and more than one half, of the arched bridge which leads from your Star-in-the-heart to her own heart centre.

She holds out her hands to you, and you set your feet on the bridge.

You realize that your feet are winged, and you find yourself floating gently over the bridge into the vast Star. And then, in great joy, you realize that the Star-in-your-heart and the great Star are one, and you are safe and at peace in the arms of Allea.

She says to you: 'Ascend the Crystal Stairway, cross the Rainbow Bridge to the heavenly realms where the angels dwell to greet us whenever you wish, but remember always to make your heart your dwelling place.'

Bathe in the glory of the eternal star, and, when you are ready, gently return over the rainbow bridge, which has become the Crystal Stairway.

Descend to the violet stair,

down to the indigo stair,

down to the blue stair,

down to the green stair,

down to the yellow stair,

down to the orange stair,

down to the red stair,

and back to earth, to the space you occupy and the here and now.

Seal your centres and, if you feel the need, root yourself into the earth by imagining strong, healthy, fibrous roots growing from the soles of your feet right down into the heart of Mother Earth.

*Claire*

# GALAXY

*T*hese few angels were as many as I had time to paint. I'd intended to do one, but could feel two, then three, then four, and even more, wanting to be painted.

✶

There are angels galore out there, Angels and Spirits, wanting to help each and every one of us.

✶

There are also Angel Spirits, Light Beings eager to help our planet as it moves towards its next phase.

✶

It's time for us to let the light in, to grow beyond restricting beliefs. Become aware of the people, books, lessons that are out there, urging us to encompass a new way of doing things. There's a whole galaxy out there, filled with all possibilities. It's time now to expand and accept what it has to offer, especially its peaceful, loving, joyous Angels.

*Olwen*

# GALAXY

These few Angels are as many as I had time to paint. I'd intended to do one, but could feel two, then three, then four and even more wanting to be painted.

There are angels galore out there. Angels and Spirits wanting to help each and everyone of us.

There are also Angel Spirits, Light Beings eager to help our planet as it moves towards its next phase. It's time for us to let the light in, to grow beyond restricted beliefs. Become aware of the people, books, lessons that are out there, urging us to encompass a new way of doing things. There's a whole galaxy out there, filled with all possibilities. It's time now to expand and accept what it has to offer, especially its peaceful, loving, joyous Angels.

*M*any people today are talking to their angels, writing to their angels, discovering their guardian angel, requesting angelic help, receiving angelic messages, marking angelic intervention in their lives, and even regularly asking their angels to find them a parking space!

All of these things are good. Yet, sometimes, perhaps even each day, it is also good to sit in stillness and quietly receive the love and the friendship of the angels, just for five minutes. We ask for nothing, communicate nothing, do nothing except open our hearts and minds to this shining inflow of healing, cleansing, reassuring angelic love. It surrounds and supports us, and lifts us into the light.

Take five. Rest in the love of the angels, and know that you are completely safe, and infinitely loved.

*Claire*

# HAVE FUN

Angels are like dolphins.
They know that there is always loads of time
to have fun, and that the more fun you have,
the more joy there is in your life
and in others.

Live life in the 90 per cent that is great, and you'll soon find
it increasing, and also find that the people in your life
are wonderful, too.

*Olwen*

# HAVE FUN

Angels are like dolphins. They know that there is always loads of time to have fun, and that the more fun you have, the more joy there is in your life and in others. Live life in the 90% that is great and you'll soon find it increasing, and also find that the people in your life are wonderful too

The angels will always nurture our sense of fun, of hilarity, of the downright ridiculous! Angels teach us to appreciate the ridiculous without ridicule. There is never any trace of cruelty or slight in their humour, although they do love to dissolve pomposity! The Spirit of Humour, which I can only describe as an effervescing angel, will suddenly appear at our side whenever an occasion is too sombre, or its energies too heavy and ponderous. It is impossible to catch the etheric eye of the Angel of Humour without wanting to collapse into fits of unrestrained laughter, even if, because of propriety, we can only laugh inside ourselves!

People who take themselves very seriously will feel uncomfortable in the presence of the Angel of Humour, not because this is what the angel intends, but because it is fostering a release into such a person's innocent and childlike nature where there is no compulsion to stand on one's dignity, and it is encountering resistance!

One of the most powerful fears we have is of being thought foolish. This fear, which is a fear of shame, is a gargantuan block on our path to freedom. What would our lives be like if we were to rid ourselves of this inner cringing and panic at the possibility that we might be considered silly?

Throw open the doors of your perception, and invite the angels of humour into your life! They will teach you to revel in and enjoy to the utmost every occasion for humour. And do not forget the fairies.

Fairies are, indeed, absolutely real, and if we ask them to show us how to introduce an element of play, an element of fun, into everything we do, they will send sparkles of gaiety and hilarity shooting into the experience of even our dullest, most mundane and oppressive tasks. Fairies entice us all the time with whispers of, 'Oh, go on. Be silly!' until our shackles fall away.

To paraphrase GK Chesterton: angels can fly because they take themselves lightly!

*Claire*

# BEAUTIFUL

These beautiful Angels are here for us, with their
beautiful and bountiful energy of Love and Joy
and Peace and Fun.

✳

They are out in the Universe as well as here
on Mother Earth.

✳

It's time that we changed our perspective and looked at what
is beautiful in our lives, really looked at what is joyous, and
at ways to have fun.

✳

How can we bring more peace into our lives and others, and
especially how can we grow in love to be more like these
beautiful Angels?

*Olwen*

## BEAUTIFUL

These beautiful Angels are here for us, with their beautiful and bountiful energy of Love and Joy and Peace and Fun

They are out in the Universe as well as here on Mother Earth.

It's time that we changed our perspective and looked at what is beautiful in our lives, really looked at what is joyous, and at ways to have fun. How can we bring more peace into our lives and others, and especially how can we grow in love to be more like these beautiful Angels?

*T*he beautiful poet and Celtic mystic, Fiona Macleod, who was both an angel visionary and a fairy-seer, came across an old man one day in her wanderings.

He was standing on the shore of one of the Scottish Western Isles, gazing out to sea, where the dawn was breaking in a wild skyscape of almost supernatural loveliness. He held his hat in both hands, and stood in reverence, with bowed head.

When Fiona Macleod addressed him, he explained to her that every day he came to this place and, taking off his hat, bowed to the spirit of beauty in nature.

Remembering her encounter with this noble old crofter, I followed his example one spring evening as I stood in my garden at sunset. What happened within the next few minutes will always remain with me.

The fiery lights in the sky took on exquisite hues of brightest angelic gold, deepest orange, lilac, violet and silver-washed, luminescent green, as well as their prevailing rose. The blue of the sky sweetened and deepened until it became ethereally lovely, as if it were some sanctified quality of spirit rather than just a colour. Then, with complete disregard to the usual orientation of the sunset, these magical jewel-like lights formed a crown, a complete ring, in the sky above my garden. They twinkled and danced and coruscated for many minutes with an angelic intensity, retaining their crown formation until, at last, the enchantment faded slowly out of the heavens.

I was left enraptured and deeply humbled. I had given a single moment of heartfelt appreciation to the spirit of beauty in nature, and had been rewarded with a breathtaking response which can only be classified in terms of an overjoyed recognition, an abundantly generous reward, and an overall expression of love - of personal love from a universal source, from the mysterious heart that beats behind the manifestation of the cosmos.

The poet Max Ehrmann wrote in his poem *The Moon*:

> I would, if I could, bring back
> into fashion the moon and the
> stars, the dawn and the sunset.
> I rarely hear anyone speak
> of them. One would think these
> perpetual wonders had
> passed from sight.

There is peace and rest in the
contemplation of these miracles
that nature paints on the
canvas of the sky.

Tonight, I looked at the moon
for a while. There was a
faint circle around it.

A friend came by and asked what
I was looking at. I pointed
to the moon.
'I don't see anything.'
'The moon,' I said.
He chuckled and went on. He will
report me as growing queer.

The mystery of the night!
And our own mystery!

Who knows what we are? No science

has yet grasped us.

The moon – the beautiful, mystical

moon – playing nightly

to empty seats!

The angels told the great twentieth-century angel seer Geoffrey Hodson:

'Those who would find us must learn to contact Nature far more intimately than is at present possible to the average person. In addition to a deeper appreciation of the beauty of Nature there must be that reverence for all her forms and moods, for all her manifold expression, which springs from a recognition of the presence of the Divine of which these forms, moods, and beauties are but the outward expression.'

*The Brotherhood of Angels and of Men* (1927)

In imagination, remove your 'hat' (a potent symbol, for in doing so we remove our mundane identity and simultaneously liberate our crown chakras) and bow to the spirit of beauty! Don't let the moon and the stars, the dancing sunlight, the ethereal heavens, the majesty of trees, the enchantment of still or moving waters, or the delight of flowers and grass, play to empty seats!

Bow to the spirit of beauty and the angels of beauty will surround you and bless you with a spiritual awakening of measureless and antiphonal delight.

*Claire*

# STANDING IN LINE

As you can see, Angels are here for us, standing in line, bringing their Divine Love and Peace and Joy and Protection to help us.

✳

Talk to them, believe in them, ask them to help. Then they will be able to stop standing in line and stand beside you and hold your hand and touch your heart.

*Olwen*

As you can see, Angels are here for us, standing in line. Bringing their Divine Love and Peace and Joy and Protection to help us.

# STANDING
# IN
# LINE

Talk to them, believe in them, ask them to help. Then they will be able to stop standing in line and stand beside you and hold your hand, and touch your heart.

The Celtic Blessing that follows is adapted from the *Carmina Gadelica*, collected and edited by Alexander Carmichael. It was said to be inspired and given to the people of the Scottish Western Isles by angels. Certainly, by softly and peacefully intoning this angel blessing prayer, the heart and the mind are attuned to the angels.

*Claire*

# Celtic Blessing

Deep peace of the running wave to you,
Deep peace of the flowing air to you,
Deep peace of the quiet earth to you,
Deep peace of the shining stars to you,
Deep peace of the sun of Peace to you.

Peace between nations,
Peace between neighbours,
Peace between lovers,
In love of the God of life.

Peace between religions,
Peace between world-views,
Peace between differences,
In love of the God of life.

Peace between races,
Peace between man and Earth,

Peace between man and beasts,
In love of the God of life.

Peace between person and person,
Peace between wife and husband,
Peace between parent and child.
In love of the God of life.

The peace of Heaven above all peace.
Bless O Heaven our hearts
Let our hearts incessantly bless,
Bless O Heaven our faces,
Let our faces bless one and all,
Bless O Heaven our eyes,
Let our eyes bless everything they see.

# TOGETHERNESS

*F*or all things the Tree of Life needs to join together to
promote growth and well being.

What we see and dislike and fear in others is also within
ourselves, it is part of life's rich pattern and it is best to
choose to live to our highest and best potential.
Yet instead of believing we are separate, superior, we need to
realize that freeing the world from fear, suffering, anger and
pain is up to us.
We do this with togetherness, the realization that we need to
unite, join hands as one.

Become light workers, growing in Spiritual strength and
joining together to support others to light up their own life.

*Olwen*

# TOGETHERNESS

For all things the tree of Life needs to join together to promote growth and well being. What we see and dislike and fear in others is also within ourselves, it is all part of life's rich pattern and it is best to choose to live to our highest and best potential.

Yet instead of believing we are separate, superior, we need to realise that freeing the world from fear, suffering, anger and pain is up to us. We do this with togetherness, the realisation that we need to unite, join hands as one. Become light workers growing in Spiritual strength and joining together to support others to light up their own life.

# THE TREE OF LIFE

Assume a relaxed meditative posture, making sure that you are comfortable and that your spine is erect and supported if necessary.

Connect with your heart centre, begin to breathe gently 'through the heart' and feel your mind gradually becoming still and serene.

Begin to see a softly radiant angelic form take shape before you. It is a mighty angel, yet its presence is comforting and reassuring. It adapts its cosmic dimensions to the eyes of your soul, and you see that it is manifesting a female orientation.

Her robes are a cascade of white light over which the hues of the rainbow reflect and play in subtle shimmering tones, ever-changing in myriad variants of the seven colour-rays. Look into her eyes, serene as blue summer skies, and let the realization wash through you that this is the Angel of Peace.

She takes you by the hand so that you step forward out of your limited everyday self and slip away with her through the shining mists of dimension into the angelic worlds.

You have come to a celestial earth, free from the constrictions of space-matter-time that encircle the physical earth, which has passed away from your awareness like a shadow and a sigh and a fleeting dream. Now you behold the earth of true reality.

It emanates such a flood of brilliant light that you can hardly register what you see before you until the angel begins to speak in a voice of calming quietude as soothing as the hush of fairweather tides. She speaks directly to you, and as her words form, the light becomes lucid, and clear images begin to rise and fall softly on your spiritual sight. 'Come with me, Dweller in the Green World, down into the deep secret places of the

Earth, down deep into her Heart. Here there is a great Light which glows like no outer sun, but rather blazes with a spiritual light so pure and lovely that mortal eyes may behold it only in dreams and visions of the spirit. It is the brilliant effulgence of Love and Joy, the supreme radiance of the Divine.

'Here in the Earth's Heart it is as if we stand in a paradise garden; and in the Garden there grows a Tree. It is the Tree of Life. We may go to it and stand at its great gnarled roots, which wind away in all directions like petrified serpents. How firmly anchored they are in the stuff of Mother Earth!

'Gaze up in wonder, Human Soul, into its fragrant boughs, garlanded in leaves tenderly glowing with a soft, peaceful, green hue, and hung with fruits of heavenly, scintillating colours sparkling with the lustre of the stars. Rainbow-coloured birds come and go among its branches, as do little birds of gentle dun earth-shades, and strange mythic animals whose fabulous colour and form you have never seen or imagined before. Each one speaks to our heart and is our brother, our sister. In joyous communion we greet one another, and our voices rise in song, for it is the Morning of the New Day.

'Yes, the dawn is breaking, and as we look up, further and deeper into the Mysteries of the Tree, we see that there are many paths upwards into its boughs, as though it were all at once a Tree and a Mountain and our soul's deepest Dream. In delight, our hearts take wing because we see that, at its very summit, the Light of the great Spirit streams forth and pours downward like a bright river of paradise deep into the Heart of the Earth where we stand, and into our own heart-vessels and into the world of sorrow below.

'Do you not see, Human Soul, that this great Tree of Life has roots not only at its base but also at its crown, and that these crown-roots are nourished by supernal worlds which may seem to you as if they vibrate at a measureless distance, but which I tell you do not lie far beyond, but rather embrace the physical Earth?

'Now, in a vision within a vision, we see ourselves moving upwards upon two of the paths which lead from the roots, up to the heavens where the Shining Ones that you call angels choir in a wonder of bliss to help and inspire you on our upward way - yours to struggle in a tomb of flesh, ours to inhabit a radiant atmosphere pulsing with Creation's joy. There is a beautiful reason that this is so, and through it a triumph to be won which is beyond imagining.

'Do not wonder, Earth Child, on beholding that path parallel to your own. It is the path I tread, the beauty-path of the angels, for just as we descend from the heights so must we also ascend again. Angels too have a path of evolution blessed by the Tree. We are always with you, and we can share worlds whenever you reach out to us and seek our presence.

'With the Staff of Life, the Pouch of Provisions and the Undying Lantern we climb, and we are never alone. Around us, everyone upon their own elected path, we see the sons and daughters of Humanity and the sons and daughters of Fairy ascending likewise; the path of Fairy is a never-ending dance of the Earth's delight, for your feet also, if you will tread it.

'Your paths cross and interweave. Fairy, angel and human beings are all linked in a Network of Light. And see how the birds of the Tree alight and dart and give forth music! They know no thresholds, but are dwellers in all three spheres.

'Now we are alone again, with the peaceful Tree stretching above us, waving its beautiful branches over our heads in benediction. Soothed, we dwell upon its shelter and protection, its kindly power and strength, the motherly perfume of its fruits and flowers, the lullabies in its rustling leaf-songs.

'Look carefully, Human Soul, for ten ineffable blossoms of the Mystical Rose are beginning to appear upon the Tree, and within each exquisite formation of fragrant petals is a winged figure. They are the Ten Divine Attributes of the perfected ManWoman, called Adam Kadmon.

'Ponder these things, for the secret of the winged figures at the heart of the blooms is one of liberation and peace for all creation.'

The Angel of Peace falls silent, and you see that she is becoming absorbed into the Tree. You understand that in a sense she is the Tree, its great supporting dynamic; and you realize that the essence of the Angel of Peace is Balance. She balances all the Ten Divine Attributes upon the Tree, and that is why she is truly the Angel of Peace. In deep quietude, she gives you her blessing.

Refreshment of soul and gladness of heart steal over you. You stroke the bark of the Tree and feel its goodness, its wholeness. Rest contemplatively beneath its spreading green boughs for a while and consider the teaching that the great Angel of Peace has offered to you as her gift.

Balance in all things is the secret of peaceful living, for all suffering is a deprivation of balance. You realize that the Tree, with its great temple-like pillars, balances all creation, and that every soul is given the opportunity to express the sacred principle of that Golden Mean of perfect balance, if it so wishes.

You look again upon the Tree of Life and see the Angel of Peace as a quiet pulse emitting her essence from its heart. The revelation comes to you that the Tree of Life is also the Tree of Peace.

Comforted, healed and ready for renewed service, you seek once more the mundane Earth of physicality below, taking with you the vivifying Light of the New Day.

Feel the solid ground beneath your feet, slowly refocus upon the things that surround you and seal your centres.

Affirm:

'All the help I need to balance my inner and outer life is available to me. I only have to ask to receive it. The Angel of Peace is in my heart and builds her temple over me.

   The roots of the Tree of Life are ever at my feet and at my crown to give me strength and peace whenever I need to draw on them.'

# GROW LOVE

Within the tree of life that you are currently living,
within its core, its centre, its heart,
grow Love.

The things that we currently count as success
are ephemeral.
Love is eternal.
Grow Love.

*Olwen*

WITHIN·THE·TREE·OF·LIFE·THAT·YOU
ARE·CURRENTLY·LIVING·WITHIN·ITS
CORE·ITS·CENTRE·ITS·HEART·GROW
LOVE·THE·THINGS·THAT·WE·CURRENTLY
COUNT·AS·SUCCESS·ARE·EPHEMERAL·
LOVE·IS·ETERNAL·GROW
·LOVE·

## ANGEL MEDITATION:
# LIVING LIGHT

Stand or sit at ease beneath a tree and perform an
act of magic that will take you into the angelic worlds.

See the white ethereal life force – purest white, brightest
white, living light itself – rising from the mystic heart
of the earth into the tree roots. Watch this delicate and
lovely light rising up the trunk, tracing each branch,
each twig, each bud, leaf and flower, with the finest
filigree of ethereal white.

Now see this enrapturing light as it reaches the highest
point of the tree. It spirals away into the heavens, its
ascension attended by angels composed of the same
softest, brightest-white light. As you contemplate the
angels, observe how the revelation of the rainbow
courses through each one, emanating flashing glimmers,
visual whispers, of the seven rays of creation.

Note how you have ascended, with the ethereal essence
of the tree, into the angelic realms!

*Claire*

# LIFE LEAVES

*A*ll the Leaves on our Tree of Life
are touched by Angels.

✳

All the leaves we see on plants and trees are connected to us
and are also connected to angels.

✳

All the Leaves in the Book of our Life have the touch of
Angels on every page.

✳

When we open ourselves to the bigger picture that
is constantly growing, our little leaves begin to glow
with potential.

*Olwen*

# LIFE LEAVES

All the Leaves on our Tree of Life are touched by Angels.

All the Leaves we see on plants and trees are connected to us and are also connected to Angels

All the Leaves in the Book of our Life have the touch of Angels on every page.

When we open ourselves to the bigger picture that is constantly growing, our little leaves begin to glow with potential.

*A* friend and I had a shared waking dream or vision. We saw that every tree, the collective presence of trees, is a living, loving symbol of God-consciousness.

We saw that the angels adore and facilitate and attend upon the spiritual and physical reality of trees, because they are indeed sacred. They are rooted into earth and into heaven.

Mighty and majestic, small and delicate, or little and shrubby, all contain the magic of the holy signature of the Tree and are worshipped by the fairies, who dance around them and in them as an expression of ritual love.

We saw that the Tree of Life, and the Tree of Knowledge of Good and Evil, are pivotal expressions of the universal God-consciousness, of Divine Intelligence. We saw that every earthly tree reflects and upholds this profoundly mysterious truth, and that lineage trees, family trees, are connected to their greater reality.

The expression of the ramification of bloodlines, of the human family, dwells within the inner mystery of the tree. The spiritual counterpart of this blood, whose physical expression is that of the living waters within us all, connects us to God-consciousness, the source and the root of all bloodlines.

We are all one, a connected, united family; and the trees show us every moment that this is so.

Little wonder, then, that the Druids and other enlightened esoteric brotherhoods (for instance, the Essenes) marked the tree as sacred, that when language and knowledge began to be widely circulated and disseminated, the wood of the tree was used to make up books out of paper, and that books consist of 'leaves'.

There is one caution the angels would extend to us in our realization of this truth. The wasp taught humanity how to make paper when we observed its pulpy, or paper, nests. Beware the sting within the leaves! The angels counsel that what we take into our minds must always be balanced by the consciousness of the heart.

All these things our dream taught us. You too might like to stand before a favourite tree and open your being in worship of this emblem of the Divine, not as an act of idolatry, of course, but as a celebration of our inner knowing, as a magnificent affirmation of our connection to God, of All That Is, of I AM THAT I AM.

Beneath the boughs of the sacred tree, intone the eternal I AM, the omnipotent AUM, for through it we strengthen and perpetually confirm that connection to God, and forge an unfailing link with the God within ourselves.

If you have ever found it rather puzzling that the name of God is I AM THAT I AM, it helps to realize that the reverse or negative-spin name or pronouncement of power is I AM NOT, the ultimate act of life-depletion! The angels advise us to keep well away from this stealer of vital force, or 'dementor', in all our thoughts, words and actions! It is surprising to note the number and range of our thoughts which betray us into this I AM NOT mentality!

It is worth remembering that the symbolism of hair teaches us that, just as we are rooted into the earth by the earth chakra beneath our feet called the Vivaxis, so are we rooted into heaven by the vitality of the crown chakra, which is directly connected to our heart centre. The fine strings of fibre we call our hair are the physical expression of the roots that connect us to heaven, to God-consciousness. Perhaps that is why red hair was associated in the past with the supreme ability to receive and ground this Divine consciousness (we are thinking here of the power of copper, the superlative conductor!).

Clearly, with the trunks of our bodies surmounted by our heads and our hair, rooted into the earth and into the heavens, we ourselves are cardinal living expressions of trees!

*Claire*

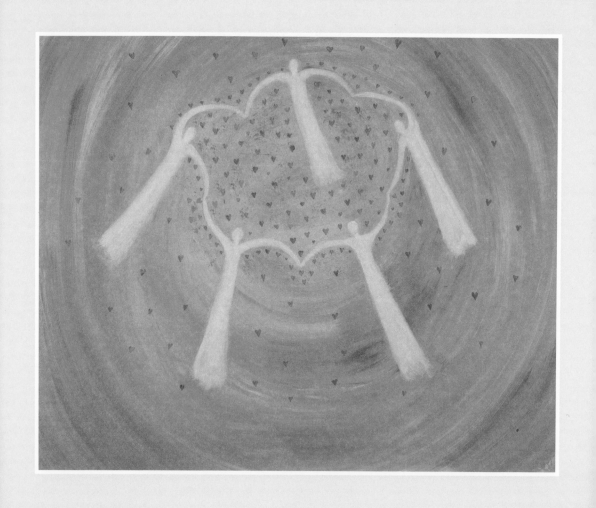

# LOVE AND JOY

*I* really would like to call this:
Love and Joy,
Joy and Love,
Love and Joy,
because if you keep saying it you can really feel the
exuberance of the Angels in the picture, who are bringing us
love, bringing us joy, bringing us peace, beauty and hope.

Open your arms, hold out your hand to the Angels and to
people. We all need a smile, a hug, our hands held.

This is how you bring the world towards the place you, your
family, and the people of the world and all the elements that
make up Mother Earth, want to exist.

*Olwen*

# LOVE AND JOY

I really would like to call this Love and Joy, Joy and Love, Love and Joy, because if you keep saying it you can really feel the exuberance of the Angels in the picture, who are bringing us love, bringing us joy, bringing us peace, beauty and hope.

Open your arms, hold out your hand to the Angels and to people. We all need a smile, a hug, our hands held.

This is how you bring the world towards the place you, your family, and the people of the world and all the elements that make up Mother Earth, want to exist.

# ANGELIC CHANTS

We can make an angelic chant by naming any positive or beautiful quality we wish to build into our soul and repeating it in rhythm.

There are three simple steps to creating an angelic chant:

Choose up to four words which express the qualities, principles or virtues you wish to absorb into your consciousness (one or two words often work better than three or four).

Choose a rhythm.

Contact the appropriate angels; for instance, if you wish to receive the angelic rays of love, beauty, peace and joy into your heart and your life, then these are the four angels to call upon.

Begin softly, musically and rhythmically to chant the words you have chosen. Summon the appropriate angel from your heart as you sound each word.

Sometimes, the angels will give you a colour or a symbol to help you absorb the desired quality or qualities. Imaginally hold up this symbol before you as you chant, or allow yourself to bathe in the colour. Occasionally, the angels will give you both a colour and a symbol.

Chant until you feel utterly at peace and at one. Then let the chant fall away into silence and contemplate the deep soothing musical harmonies within the sacred silence.

Gently emerge from your meditation and seal your chakras. Thank the angels.

*Claire*

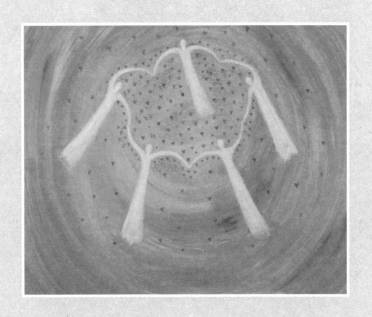

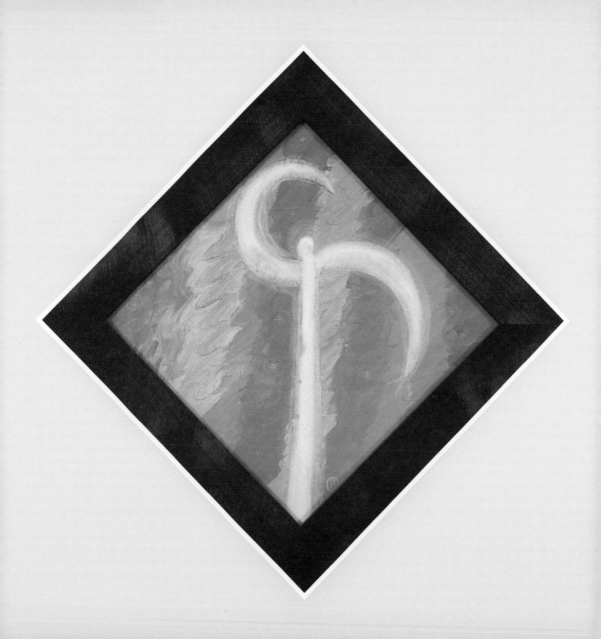

# WAVES OF ENERGY

*A*re you sending out waves of light energy to raise consciousness on Mother Earth, and are you open to receive that light in return?

✳

Like this angel reaching out, above and below, are you open to your true and magnificent potential?

✳

Are you doing your best for your mind, body and spirit, because then you can do the best for everyone and everything you come into contact with?

✳

Angels are sending us waves of Love, Peace, Joy, Friendship, Trust, waves of positive energy. It's time for the vast majority of people on Earth to increase their output of positive energy, starting NOW!

*Olwen*

WAVES
of
ENERGY

Are you sending out waves
of light energy to raise consciousness
on Mother Earth, and are you open
to receive that light in return?

Like this Angel
reaching out, above and below, are you open to
your true and magnificent potential? Are you
doing your best for your mind, body and spirit,
because then you can do the best for everyone and
and everything you come into contact with?

Angels are sending us
waves
of
Love, Peace, Joy, Friendship, Trust, waves of
positive energy. It's time for the vast majority
of people on Earth to increase their
output of positive energy starting

NOW.

*T*he wave-form is fundamental to life. Via its undulations we receive the idea of the Divine Serpent or Dragon. Vilified for many ages, and cast into the role of the 'devil', it is time to rediscover the Divine Dragon within and allow ourselves to become consummate with it.

This noble and majestic creature is not the writhing serpent of the lower self, but the mighty Being of Light which dwells in our innermost core and which overcomes and subsumes the angry creature that drives the energies and inclinations of the lower mind.

When we are in the coils of the lower dragon, in the grip of the lower nature, we are in truth caught up in the undisciplined and unharmonized energy of one or more of the chakras other than the heart.

To return to this vital heart centre, in which the true Dragon of our greater self dwells, we have to make a sacrifice. We must consciously sacrifice our anger or our stubbornness, our pride or our overriding sense of being right, or perhaps the fierceness of a selfish desire.

It is a little act, preceded by no great fanfare, performed quietly within the privacy of our own being. And yet it is supremely powerful. As if by magic, we are ushered back into the quietude of the heart, where our being is once more poised in the radiance of the star which shines within this chakra.

From the centre of that star, our Dragon form can begin to emerge – the Divine or Pendragon – for the Dragon at our heart is a being born of the sacred starlight.

Put on your Pendragon form with courage and spiritual triumph! Feel the empowerment as your Dragon self reaches for the light and unites with it.

When we are one with the Divine Dragon within, we resonate with the angels.

*Claire*

# PINK LOVE

Angels are energy, and we are especially blessed that we
can ask them to share their energy with us.

✳

When we ask for the beautiful pink love energy to flow
through us, we can also join hands and let it flow through us
into others.

✳

What a gift, what a joy, what a reason to give thanks and
marvel at the wonder of it all!

*Olwen*

# PINK LOVE

Angels are energy, and we are especially blessed that we can ask them to share their energy with us. What a gift, what a joy, what a reason to give thanks and marvel at the wonder of it all!

When we ask for the beautiful pink love energy to flow through us, we can also join hands and let it flow through us into others.

*T*he meditation poem that follows concerns the mystic rose in our heart centre. This pink rose is our heart of hearts. It is from this point that we link with the angels.

## The Rose in the Heart

Find the point of peace within.
It dwells not in the mind,
Not in the turbulent emotional body,
But deep in the heart, like a tranquil jewel.

Give up the haughty claims of the mind,
Give up the anxiety-spell of the emotional body:
Go straight to the heart.

Like a babe enfolded in the embrace of its mother,
Peace will hold you in everlasting arms;
It is a rose softly lit with the light of eternity.
Within its temple you receive true Selfhood.
Your in-breath partakes of its holy essence.
You breathe out its fragrance to heal the world.

*Claire*

# DAYBREAK

Angels are with you through the night.
Angels are there for you at daybreak.
Angels support you until sunset, and again are with you
through the night.
Let this be a breakthrough moment for you.
Embrace this knowledge like an awakening day.
Allow this light of awakening to shine into the core
of your being.
This light knows that you can talk with Angels
during every moment of your life.
Wow!

*Olwen*

# DAYBREAK

Angels are with you through the night.

Angels are there for you at daybreak.

Angels support you until sunset, and again are with you through the night.

Let this be a breakthrough moment for you.

Embrace this knowledge like an awakening day.

Allow this light to shine into the core of your being.

This light knows that you can talk with Angels during every moment of your life.

Wow!

# Abou Ben Adhem

Abou Ben Adhem (may his tribe increase!)
Awoke one night from a deep dream of peace,
And saw, within the moonlight in his room
Making it rich, and like a lily bloom,
An Angel writing in a book of gold:

Exceeding peace had made Ben Adhem bold,
And to the presence in the room he said,
'What writest thou?' The vision raised its head,
And with a look made of all sweet accord,
Answered, 'The names of those who love the Lord.'

'And mine is one?' said Abou. 'Nay, not so,'
Replied the Angel. Abou spoke more low,
But cheerily still; and said, 'I pray thee, then,
Write me as one that loves his fellow men.'
The Angel wrote, and vanished. The next night
It came again with a great awakening light,
And showed the names of those who love of God had blest;
And lo! Ben Adhem's name led all the rest.

*James Henry Leigh Hunt*

# ANGEL
# ACROSTIC

*O*lwen has designed the following five angelic encounters to form an acrostic of the word 'angel'.

*A*re You Ready?

*N*ow's the Time

*G*o For It

*E*veryone Can Do It

*L*et There Be Love

# ARE YOU READY?

We are all boxed, by our childhood, by our experiences,
by our job or lack of one.

✻

If you really want to move, if you are ready, ask your Angels
to help.

✻

The four you see here are just about to help you break out.
So Are You Ready?

✻

Yes, of course you are!

*Olwen*

ARE YOU READY

We
are
all
boxed
by our
childhood
by our

experiences,
by our job or
lack of one. If
you really want
to move, if you are
ready, ask your Angels
to help.

The four you see here are
just about to help you
break out. So Are You Ready?
Yes,
of course you
are.

*If you really want to move,*

*if you are ready,*

*ask your Angels to help.*

# NOW'S THE TIME

*W*e can all listen to the negativity being pumped at us from all sides.

✳

Or we can look at the unsung heroes we know doing super things for others. We can look at the profoundly beautiful things being produced in abundance and diversity. We can look at nature and all its blessings.

✳

What we think about is what happens, so now is the time to break out of the negativity box, and think big and beautiful things, to grow our own lives and so the world into the wonderful place it's intended to be.

*Olwen*

# NOW'S THE TIME

We can all listen to the negativity being pumped at us from all sides.

Or we can look at the unsung heroes we know doing super things for others. We can look at the profoundly beautiful things being produced in abundance and diversity. We can look at nature and all its blessings.

What we think about is what happens, so now is the time to break out of the negativity box, and think big and beautiful things to grow our own lives and so the world into the wonderful place it's intended to be.

Now's the time

to break out of the negativity box,

and think big and beautiful things,

to grow our own lives and so the world

into the wonderful place

it's intended to be.

# GO FOR IT!

We know that there are areas within us
that are still boxed.

✳

We know that we can ask Angels to help us break through
the restrictions that we and others place on ourselves.

✳

The boundaries we place are just thoughts, standing like
walls around us, appearing solid, but if we ask for help to
change those thoughts, they start to dissolve.

✳

Go for it! Ask your Angels for a breakthrough, so you can
grow and improve, and know the beauty of life without self-
imposed walls.

*Olwen*

# GO FOR IT

We know there are
areas within us that
are still boxed. We know that we can
ask Angels to help us break through
the restrictions we and others place
on ourselves.
 The boundaries we place are just
thoughts, standing like walls around
us, appearing
solid, but
if we
 ask
 for help to change
 those thoughts
 they start to
 dissolve.

Go for it!
Ask your Angels for a break-through,
so you can grow and improve,
and know the beauty of
life without self-imposed walls.

*Go for it !*

*Ask your Angels for a breakthrough,*

*so you can grow and improve, and know the beauty*

*of life without self-imposed walls.*

# EVERYONE CAN DO IT

*W*e can all change. You hear people talking as if things are set in stone; they are not.

✳

Even if we feel they are, that our upbringing, our circumstances, our problems with our family, appear to be rock solid and inescapable, we as individuals have the key.

✳

If you don't like the box you are in, if you don't like the path you are walking, if you don't like your job, the way your family and friends treat you, or where you live, it can all change and it begins with you.

✳

This picture is about asking your Angels to help you and support your changing and breaking out of the box.

✳

# EVERYONE CAN DO IT

We can all change. You
hear people talking as
if things are set in stone and they are
not. Even if we feel they are, that our
upbringing, our circumstances, our
family, appear to be rock solid, we as
individuals have the key.
If you don't like the box you are in,
if you don't like the path you are
walking, if you don't like your job,
the way your family and friends
treat you or where you live, it can
all change and it begins with you.
This picture is about asking your
Angels to help you and support your
changing and breaking out of the
box.
The whole of the human race here on
earth depends on you, on each and
every individual learning Peace and
Love, and Joy, and kindness and
Freedom from Fear. We each decide
what the World will be like by living that
life ourselves.

The whole of the human race here on earth depends on you, on each and every individual learning Peace and Love, and Joy, and Kindness, and Freedom from Fear.

✳

We each decide what the world will be like by living that life ourselves.

*Olwen*

# LET THERE BE LOVE

All religions talk about Love, yet over the centuries have waged war. Whatever must God think! I'm sure any parent would want their children to live in Love and Peace and Joy and freedom from fear.

✳

We have a world where there is an abundance of food and clothing and housing. Let there be love enough for us to tell our governments that we want to stop overeating in the countries that are able to, and to make sure that everyone has their daily bread and shelter.

✳

'Let there be Love' starts with each of us being loving with our family, our friends and ourselves. Then we need to look at the people we find difficult and look for something to love about them. The more love we give, the more we receive, and the more love grows in the world.

✳

LET THERE BE LOVE

All religions talk about Love yet over the centuries have waged war. Whatever must God think! I'm sure any parent would want their children to live in Love and Peace and Joy and Freedom from fear. We have a World where there is an abundance of food and clothing and housing. Let there be love enough for us to tell our governments that we want to stop overeating in the countries that are able to, and to make sure that everyone has their daily bread and shelter. 'Let there be love' starts with each of us being loving with our family, our friends and ourselves. Then we need to look at the people we find difficult and look for something to Love about them. The more love we give, the more we receive; and the more Love grows in the World.

Ask the Angels to help. They are filled with Love, and eager to help us now.

Ask the Angels to help.
They are filled with Love,
and eager to help us now.

*Olwen*

# THE BLESSING ANGELS

Whatever we do, whatever enterprise we undertake, however humble or exalted, the blessing angels will lend their grace and facilitation to our task.

We have only to ask. We must remember to ask, because angels will never override our free will. They wait for a conscious invitation to act on our behalf.

If we always make a point of summoning the blessing angels in everything we do, we can rest assured that circumstances will conspire to produce the highest good, even if we have to wait a while before we can recognize each positive outworking.

Call on the blessing angels. They never tire or grow impatient of our requests, because they are an eternally replenished source. It is their joy and delight to give us their gift of benediction.

Make the angels happy! Ask for their blessing!

*Claire*